APPOINTMENT IN VENICE

ALSO BY ALEX GOTFRYD

EGYPT: THE ETERNAL SMILE
Reflections on a Journey
with Allen Drury

APPOINTMENT IN VENICE

ALEX GOTFRYD

DOUBLEDAY

NEW YORK LONDON TORONTO SYDNEY AUCKLAND

Published by Doubleday, a division of
Bantam Doubleday Dell Publishing Group, Inc.,
666 Fifth Avenue, New York, New York 10103.

Doubleday and the portrayal of an anchor with a dolphin
are trademarks of Doubleday, a division of
Bantam Doubleday Dell Publishing Group, Inc.

Library of Congress Cataloging-in-Publication Data
Gotfryd, Alex.
Appointment in Venice /Alex Gotfryd.—1st ed.
p.   cm.
1. Venice (Italy)—Description—1981—Views.   I. Title.
DG674.7G67 1988
945'.31—dc19   88-14007
ISBN 0-385-24841-5

HR

FOR
NANCY EVANS

ACKNOWLEDGMENTS

With deepest gratitude to Lynn Kohlman and Gabrielle von Canal
for their sensitive participation,
to Alberto Vitale for his kind support,
to J. C. Suarès for his visual wisdom, to Peter Kruzan for his invaluable help,
to Ellen Violett and Carolyn Blakemore for their wise suggestions,
to Mary Homi and Dr. Natale Rusconi of the Cipriani, Venice, for their generosity,
and finally to C. G. Jung's *Memories, Dreams, Reflections,*
the reading of which triggered my own "confrontation with the subconscious."

These are the images of an actual dream,
the kind that recurs,
evoking certain appointments one has in a lifetime,
always leading up to the last one

The images in this book are those of a dream I had three months after the death of my father. The setting was Venice, a city I had visited twice—many years apart—once in the summer and once in the fall. The summer visit, a long time ago, impressed me deeply, but it appeared to me as a city full of transients, people on the way to somewhere else. I was struck by a sense of carnival and decided to come back at a more sober time, perhaps in the fall or winter. Years later I fulfilled that promise and returned to Venice in October. It was a melancholy time of life for me and this extraordinary city suited my temperament at that moment. I had a chance to savor it alone, without the interference of summer crowds. It rained most of the time, and this fog-enveloped place had a mesmerizing effect.

I would wake up by five a.m. and start exploring an hour later. The city was still asleep except for a few street sweepers at St. Mark's Place. I could barely see their moving silhouettes emerging from the morning mist. By seven o'clock the city was beginning to come to life, the fog began to lift, and the spell was broken. The hour between six and seven a.m. was hypnotic—it was not of this world, and it belonged to me, powerful and soundless, forever burned into my subconscious.

Now, years later, these haunting moments emerged in the form of a dream. The locale was Venice; the time, that magic time in the fall. The dream emerging from the Venice fog, appearing and disappearing like the fog, was a full scenario in the same sequence as these photographs. As a photographer, I was impressed with the visual allure and iconography, and the somnambulistic, almost underwater quality. I thought about it for a while and then went ahead with the everydayness of my life. A week later, the dream recurred. This time I wrote it down in my notebook. Not a day passed that I did not think about it. It became an obsession.

Why was I dreaming this dream?

Who is the woman in black?

Who is the other woman?

Who is the man?

Being of an analytical nature, I knew that the dream was symbolic. The existential aspect of the symbolism was not entirely foreign to me. You go through life alone—the people you meet are narcissistic images of yourself—relationships don't last—affairs are mutual delusions and distractions from death. You end up having breakfast alone. You take the boat to nowhere, knock on the door, and confront yourself. Ultimately, you are responsible to yourself, for yourself. Then darkness. I perceived the dream as one of frustrated hopes, lost illusions, and the inevitability of the human condition.

This was my journey into the subconscious—a land of was, is, and will be, illuminating a hidden crystallized truth, a moment of time lost, perhaps a moment of time that never happened, and perhaps time to come, merging and recording images forever young, never to age, reflecting the anxiety of all time by means of flashbacks and flashforwards. I found myself in the essence of time—and at the same time I was outside of it, suspended, looking into despair and the abyss.

One day on an assignment, when I was photographing Lynn Kohlman, a beautiful model and a photographer herself, I found myself blurting out, "Let's go to Venice for two weeks and photograph my dream." Lynn, a good friend, agreed without a moment's hesitation. I later mentioned the project to another friend, also a fashion model, Gabrielle von Canal, who told me that she would be in Milan in November and could join us in Venice for three days, to shoot her sequence. I now could photograph my dream, my obsession.

Venice in November was just as I expected it would be—immersed in fog and the mystery of time. We rose every morning at four to prepare for all exterior photography, which began at five-thirty while the city still slept. By seven we stopped, as the light became less ephemeral. Interior shots were done later in the day. It was an intensive two-week schedule. We succeeded in completing our work a day before our departure for New York. At last the dream was photographed.

The entire experience was so deeply emotional and draining that upon my return, all I could do was to develop the film. For months I could not face editing the photographs. Surprisingly, when I finally did begin to edit them, I found that the images fell into their proper sequence. Now the dream was with me constantly—the photographic images imprinted on my brain. They became an overwhelming presence, evidence of the dream's reality. I felt compelled to look at them often, ritualistically, listening to a Vivaldi oboe concerto. The plaintive sound of the oboe made the experience even more powerful and melancholy.

At the suggestion of a friend, I took the photographs to a well-known psycho-analyst. I had alerted him on the phone that I did not want to be analyzed but would appreciate a few sessions to discuss the dream as I had photographed it.

"I brought you my dream," I said, as I began to display the photographs in sequence.

He asked me what I thought the dream meant. As I began talking, he interrupted, "Who is this woman in black?" Somehow I was at a loss for words. "I don't know—every woman…every man…an aspect of me?"

He then said, "Tell me about your mother?"

"She was killed when I was very young in Auschwitz."

We talked some more—about my years spent in concentration camps. Suddenly the fifty-minute hour was over. I collected my portfolio and left his office, never to return.

A month later my aunt, my mother's sister, arrived from Europe for a two-week visit. After I had shown her my Venice dream, she looked at me with eyes filled with tears and said, "Darling, that woman in black, she looks just like your mother."

APPOINTMENT IN VENICE

PLATE 1

PLATE 2

PLATE 3

PLATE 4

PLATE 5

PLATE 6

PLATE 7

PLATE 8

PLATE 9

PLATE 10

PLATE 11

PLATE 12

PLATE 13

PLATE 14

PLATE 15

PLATE 16

PLATE 17

PLATE 18

PLATE 19

PLATE 20

PLATE 21

PLATE 22

PLATE 23

PLATE 24

PLATE 25

PLATE 26

PLATE 27

PLATE 28

PLATE 29

PLATE 30

PLATE 31

PLATE 32

PLATE 33

PLATE 34

PLATE 35

PLATE 36

PLATE 37

PLATE 38

PLATE 39

PLATE 40

PLATE 41

PLATE 42

PLATE 43